The 3-D Library of the Human Body

THE BRAIN AND SPINAL CORD

LEARNING HOW WE THINK, FEEL, AND MOVE

Chris Hayhurst

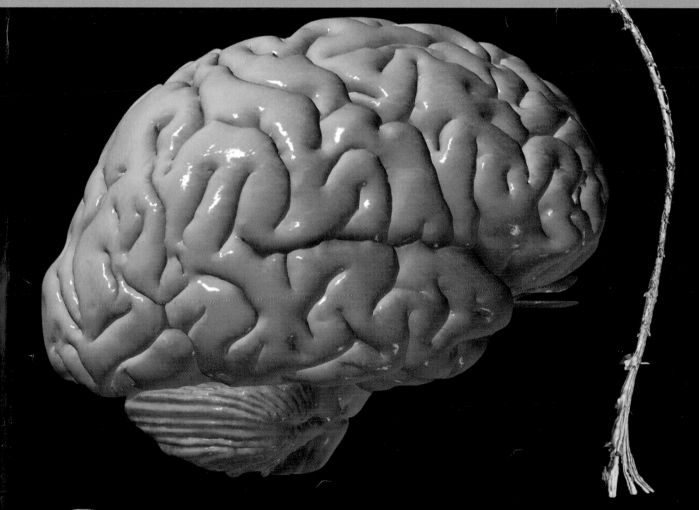

the rosen publishing group's
rosen
central

Editor's Note

The idea for the illustrations in this book originated in 1986 with the Vesalius Project at Colorado State University's Department of Anatomy and Neurobiology. There, a team of scientists and illustrators dreamed of turning conventional two-dimensional anatomical illustrations into three-dimensional computer images that could be rotated and viewed from any angle, for the benefit of students of medicine and biology. In 1988 this dream became the Visible Human Project™, under the sponsorship of the National Library of Medicine in Bethesda, Maryland. A grant was awarded to the University of Colorado School of Medicine, and in 1993 the first work of dissection and scanning began on the body of a Texas convict who had been executed by lethal injection. The process was repeated on the body of a Maryland woman who had died of a heart attack. Applying the latest techniques of computer graphics, the scientific team was able to create a series of three-dimensional digital images of the human body so beautiful and startlingly accurate that they seem more in the realm of art than science. On the computer screen, muscles, bones, and organs of the body can be turned and viewed from any angle, and layers of tissue can be electronically peeled away to reveal what lies underneath. In reproducing these digital images in two-dimensional print form, the editors at Rosen have tried to preserve the three-dimensional character of the work by showing organs of the body from different perspectives and using illustrations that progressively reveal deeper layers of anatomical structure.

Published in 2002 by The Rosen Publishing Group, Inc.
29 East 21st Street, New York, NY 10010

Copyright © 2002 by The Rosen Publishing Group, Inc.

All digital anatomy images copyright © 1999 by Visible Productions.

Digital anatomy images published by arrangement with Anatographica, LLC.
216 East 49th Street, New York, NY 10017

First Edition

Library of Congress Cataloging-in-Publication Data

Hayhurst, Chris.
The brain and spinal cord: learning how we think, feel, and move / Chris Hayhurst.
p. cm. — (The 3-D library of the human body)
Includes bibliographical references and index.
Summary: A discussion of the anatomy and physiology of the human brain and spinal cord, the structure of the nervous system, and how we think, feel, and move.
ISBN 0-8239-3528-0
1. Central nervous system—Juvenile literature. [1. Brain. 2. Nervous system.]
I. Title. II. Series.
QP361.5 .H39 2001
612.8—dc21
                                                                    2001002993

Manufactured in the United States of America

CONTENTS

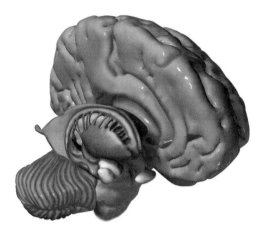

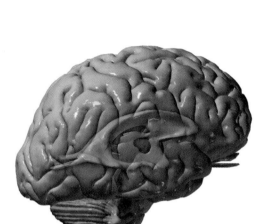

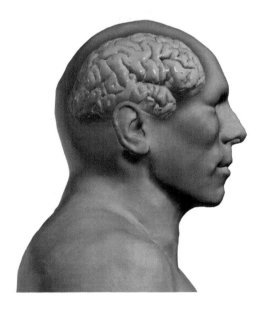

PREFACE
ANESTHESIA

The effective treatment of illness often requires surgery, and surgery was simply not practical before the appearance of drugs to relieve pain. Before the middle of the nineteenth century, surgery was seen only as a last resort and an act of desperation that killed as many patients as it cured. Doctors who recorded their impressions of surgery before painkillers describe scenes of screaming reminiscent of the medieval torture chamber. And yet many people, including some doctors, were not entirely comfortable with efforts to alleviate pain. Wasn't pain the Lord's punishment for the wicked and a trial for the righteous? Didn't the Bible say of women and childbirth, "In sorrow thou shalt bring forth children"? In the late sixteenth century, a woman in Edinburgh, Scotland, was buried alive for seeking relief from the pain of childbirth from another woman accused of witchcraft.

Drugs like laudanum, a mixture of opium and alcohol, had been around for a long time. In 1800, English chemist Humphrey Davy suggested the use of nitrous oxide as a painkiller. In 1803, Frederich Wilhelm Seturner (1783–1841) isolated crystals of morphine from crude opium, but it could not be administered effectively until the invention of the syringe in the 1850s. In 1897, Felix Hoffman, working for the German firm Bayer, developed the compound acetylsalicylic acid, which was marketed as a painkiller under the trade name Aspirin. All of these substances, however, had drawbacks. They were either not strong enough for surgical procedures, difficult to administer in the right doses, or they induced unpleasant side effects.

Ether, a compound made from sulfuric acid and alcohol, was discovered by the Spanish chemist Raymundus Lullius in 1275, but it was centuries before its anesthetic properties were recognized. The first use of ether as a surgical anesthetic was by the American surgeon Dr. Crawford Williams Long (1815–1878) on March 30, 1842, when he removed two tumors from the neck of a patient. Dr. Long performed eight more operations using ether in the following years, but he did not publish his results until 1849. For this reason, the credit for the first use of ether as an anesthetic has gone to another American, Dr. William Thomas Green Morton (1819–1868).

Dr. Morton was a dentist, and early in 1846 he began to experiment with ether at his home in West Needham, Massachusetts, dosing not only small animals but himself. In September of that year, in his Boston office, he used ether to painlessly extract a tooth from a patient. Local press reports of his success brought Morton to the attention of Dr. John Collins Warren, senior surgeon at Massachusetts General Hospital. On the morning of October 16, 1846, Dr. Morton brought his ether apparatus to Dr. Warren's operating theater at Mass General and anesthetized Edward Gilbert Abbott, a twenty-year-old man with a tumor in his neck. "Your patient is ready, sir," said Dr. Morton, and Dr. Warren then successfully removed the tumor. After the procedure, Dr. Warren turned to the prestigious group of doctors in the gallery and said, "Gentlemen, this is no humbug." Painless surgery had arrived. Shortly after the demonstration, Oliver Wendell Holmes (1809–1894), a professor of anatomy soon to become dean of Harvard Medical School, wrote to Morton and suggested the name "anesthesia" for the state of unconsciousness induced by ether.

Almost immediately afterward, the Scottish physician James Young Simpson (1811–1870) tried to substitute chloroform for ether because of ether's disagreeable odor. In the long term he was not successful, because chloroform is more volatile and difficult to handle safely, but he did perform a number of painless procedures using chloroform, most of them attempts to alleviate the pain of childbirth. Here he encountered religious prejudice against the use of anesthetics during childbirth. But in 1853, Queen Victoria appointed Simpson her personal physician and chose to be anesthetized for the births of her seventh and eighth children. As a result, the prejudice against anesthetics quickly fell away, and in upper- and middle-class families painless childbirth became quite common.

1
THE BRAIN

What weighs about three pounds, is the size of a large grapefruit, and is the most complex organ in the human body? The answer's in your head: the brain.

The human brain is an incredibly important piece of anatomical machinery. Your body would be completely useless without it. You couldn't read this book. Writing would be impossible. You'd have no memory, no thoughts, no emotions, and no way to breathe. You couldn't see, feel, sleep, eat, walk, talk, or log onto the Internet. You need your brain for absolutely everything you do.

Were you to crack your skull wide open, pull your brain out, and cradle it in your hands, first off, you'd be dead. But if, for educational purposes only, you did survive, you'd see a slimy, lumpy, pinkish-gray mass of mush. It would look a lot like a gray walnut, only much bigger, far heavier, and a lot less appetizing.

Brain Protection

Since it's such a vital organ, the brain is guarded from harm by no less than five protective layers. The first and outermost layer, and the one mentioned above, is the skull. The skull surrounds the brain like a permanent and perfectly fitted bicycle helmet. It's hard, sturdy, and a great first defense against everyday bangs and bumps. The skull is the brain's brick wall—its main coat of armor, so to speak.

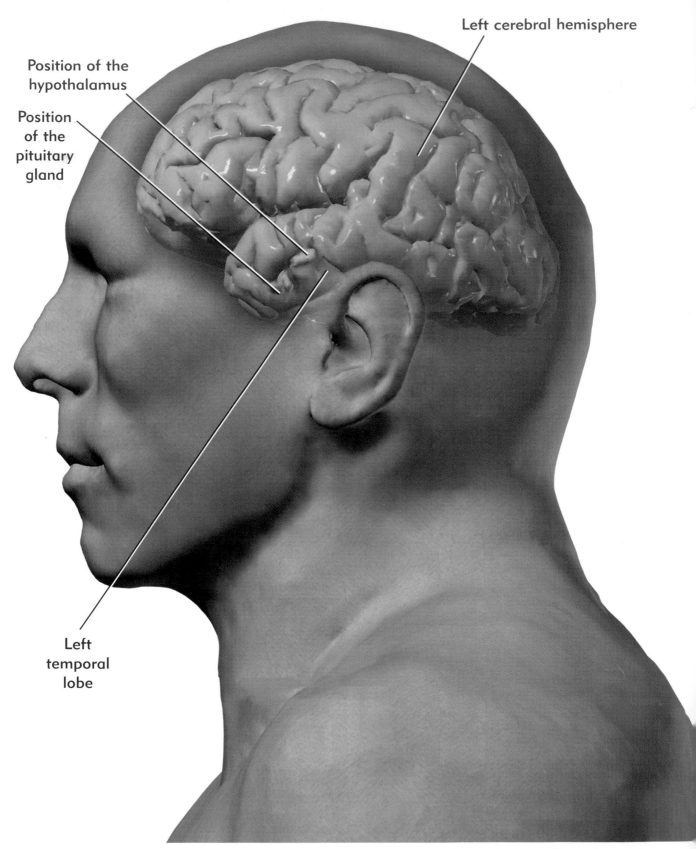

Left cerebral hemisphere

Position of the hypothalamus

Position of the pituitary gland

Left temporal lobe

The brain is the most important organ in the body, so it is well protected within the skull.

The brain's next three layers of protection are known collectively as meninges. The meninges are separate sheets of body tissue that stack up one on top of the other. The outer strip, a tough membrane attached to the inside of the skull, is known as the dura mater ("dura mater" means "tough mother" in Latin). Beneath that is the middle meningeal layer, called the arachnoid. Below the arachnoid—and separated from it by a narrow gap known as the subarachnoid space—is the third meningeal layer, the pia mater, which clings to the brain and all its numerous pits (sulci) and folds (gyri) like plastic wrap on a chunk of raw hamburger.

Last among the brain's physical protectors, but certainly not least, is a clear, waterlike substance known as cerebrospinal fluid. It is produced by the brain's vascular system and circulates within the subarachnoid space. It acts like a liquid cushion between the brain and the skull.

Brain Anatomy

Beneath the meningeal layers is the real meat of the brain. There are three main parts: the cerebrum, the cerebellum, and the brain stem.

The cerebrum is the brain's largest component, accounting for most of its weight and nearly three-fourths of its volume. It forms the top of the brain and is the control center for thoughts, feelings, sensations, and voluntary actions. The hills and valleys of the cerebrum are covered by a layer of tissue called the cerebral cortex, and the cerebrum is physically divided into two halves by a deep, canyonlike groove called the longitudinal fissure. The left side of the split is known as the left cerebral hemisphere. The right half is called the right cerebral hemisphere.

Each hemisphere consists of four rounded cerebral lobes, or regions. The lobes are named after the particular skull bones that protect them and, like the cerebral hemispheres, are separated by fissures. The frontal lobes are located in the front, or ventral, portion of each hemisphere.

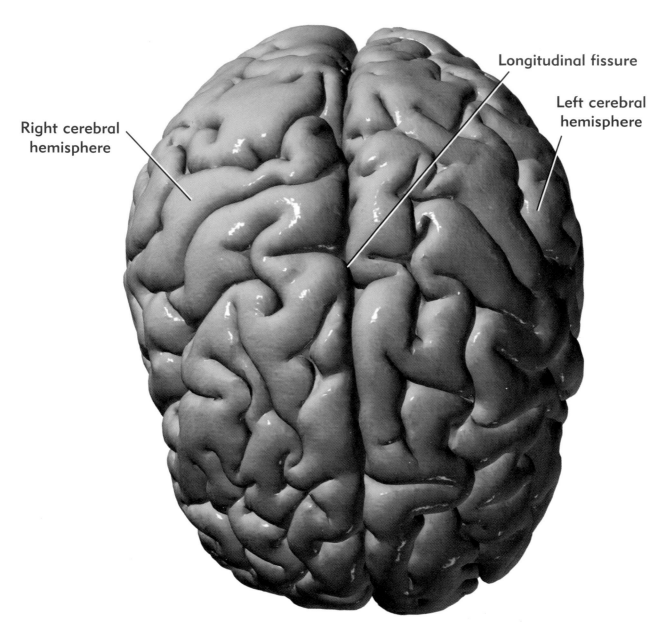

Longitudinal fissure

Left cerebral hemisphere

Right cerebral hemisphere

A superior (from above) view of the cerebral cortex, the gray matter in which conscious thinking takes place. The front of the brain is at the bottom of the image.

Parietal lobes are medial—that is, they're near the middle. Occipital lobes are dorsal, or in the back. Temporal lobes are lateral and inferior, or along the bottom sides. The central sulcus (a deep fissure) divides the frontal and parietal lobes, while the lateral sulcus separates the temporal lobe from the parietal and frontal lobes.

In order for the two hemispheres to function efficiently with one another, they must be connected, and that job goes to the corpus callosum. The corpus callosum is an arching network of fibers that bridges the hemispheres from its location just above the brain stem. By linking the hemispheres together, it allows them to communicate and cooperate with each other. So when information is received by or sent from one hemisphere, the other hemisphere knows all about it.

A second major brain part, the cerebellum, lies inferior and dorsal to the cerebrum's occipital lobe. "Cerebellum" comes from the Latin word for "little brain," and that's exactly what it is—a miniature version of the cerebrum, which most people think of as "the brain." The cerebellum is responsible for unconscious movements—things such as breathing, blinking, and coordination. By interpreting information gathered from the eyes and the ears, it allows us to keep our form and balance and move our muscles exactly when and how we want to move them. Like the cerebrum, the cerebellum is divided into left and right hemispheres and has an irregularly shaped surface.

The last of the three main brain divisions is the brain stem, which connects the cerebrum to the spinal cord. About three inches long, the width of a carrot, and shaped like a funnel, it sticks out from the inferior end of the cerebrum much like the stalk of a plant might protrude from a flower. The brain stem has four major parts: the medulla oblongata, the pons, the midbrain, and the diencephalon.

The medulla oblongata is at the most inferior end of the brain stem and is continuous with the spinal cord. It houses nerve centers that control the body's breathing, heart rate, blood pressure, swallowing, and other important functions. Above the medulla oblongata is the pons. The bulbous, rounded pons has millions of microscopic, threadlike nerve fibers. The smallest part of the brain stem is the midbrain. The midbrain rests just above the pons and helps control eye movement and

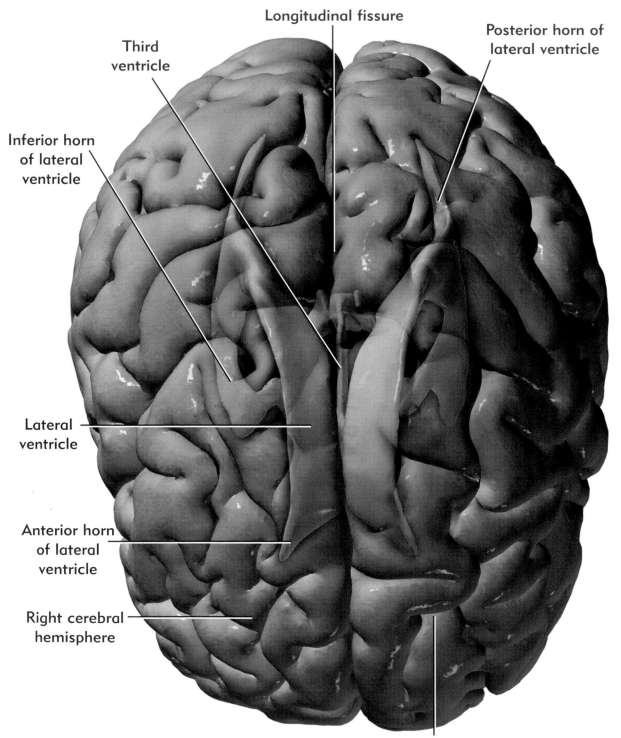

Third
ventricle

Longitudinal fissure

Posterior horn of
lateral ventricle

Inferior horn
of lateral
ventricle

Lateral
ventricle

Anterior horn
of lateral
ventricle

Right cerebral
hemisphere

Left cerebral hemisphere

This view of the brain reveals the division of its hemispheres and the fissured cerebral cortex. The ventricles contain cerebrospinal fluid that nourishes and protects the brain.

hearing. Finally, at the top of the brain stem, sandwiched between the midbrain and the cerebrum, is the diencephalon. The various parts of the diencephalon, like the thalamus, hypothalamus, and epithalamus, regulate internal body conditions like temperature and hunger. They also receive sensory nerve impulses, or sensations, from the rest of the body and relay them to the cerebrum.

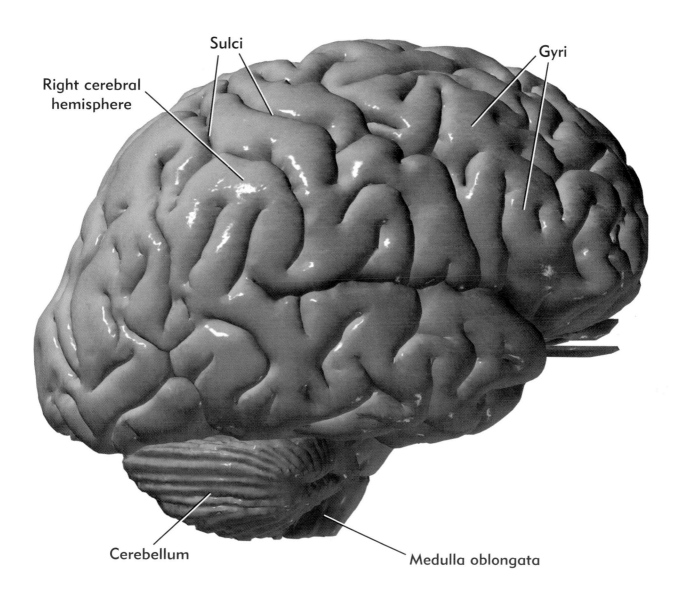

The sulci (pits) and gyri (folds) of the cerebral cortex give it a large surface area and allow a lot of brain tissue to be squeezed into the skull.

The Ventricular System

Ventricles are cavities or chambers inside the brain that produce and circulate cerebrospinal fluid. The brain has four ventricles. Two of the ventricles, one in each of the cerebral hemispheres, are referred to as lateral ventricles. The other two are known as the third and fourth ventricles. The third ventricle is located in the diencephalon. The fourth ventricle is below the third ventricle. Most cerebrospinal fluid is produced in the two lateral ventricles by a structure called the choroid plexus. From there, it flows into the third ventricle, where it is joined by more cerebrospinal fluid. It then continues on to the fourth ventricle through a narrow tunnel called the cerebral aqueduct. Once in the fourth ventricle, it combines with the cerebrospinal fluid produced there. Finally, most of the cerebrospinal fluid leaves the ventricular system through holes in the fourth ventricle and enters the subarachnoid space—the space between the arachnoid and the pia mater. From the subarachnoid space the cerebrospinal fluid spreads out to bathe the entire surface of the brain and the spinal cord. Cerebrospinal fluid is constantly produced by the ventricles and, at the same time, drained back into the bloodstream through venous sinuses. In a healthy human body, cerebrospinal fluid is constantly circulating at all times.

The Vascular System of the Brain

The brain, more than any other organ in the human body, needs blood—and the oxygen and nutrients that are in it—to survive. Without oxygen, brain cells would starve and die in just a few minutes. To ensure that the brain doesn't run out of oxygen, the heart does everything and anything to supply it with sufficient amounts of blood. In fact, if necessary, the heart will deliver blood to the brain at the expense of any other organ in the body.

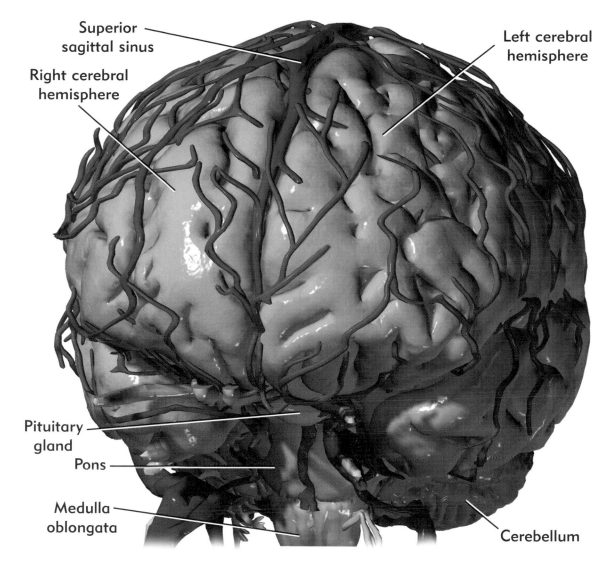

Superior
sagittal sinus

Right cerebral
hemisphere

Left cerebral
hemisphere

Pituitary
gland

Pons

Medulla
oblongata

Cerebellum

Arteries and veins carry blood throughout the brain's cerebral hemispheres, the brain stem, and the cerebellum.

Arteries and veins are part of the body's vascular system. Arteries carry oxygen-rich blood from the heart to the brain, while veins circulate oxygen-poor blood back to the heart. The heart then pumps the venous blood out to the lungs—where the exchange of oxygen-poor blood for highly oxygenated blood occurs—before redirecting it to all other body parts, including the brain.

2

THE SPINAL CORD

Like all good leaders, the brain works best as part of a team. Accordingly, the brain's partner is the spinal cord. The spinal cord is a long, narrow, white cable of nerves that acts like the brain's internal mailman. It delivers messages and information back and forth between the brain and the rest of the body.

The superior, or top, end of the spinal cord meets the base of the brain at the brain stem. The inferior end is located about two-thirds of the way down the spinal column. The spinal column is what most of us know as the backbone. The bony spinal column surrounds the spinal cord like a sheath and helps protect it from injury.

The Spinal Column

To understand the spinal cord, it helps to know a little about the spinal column. The spinal column, which anatomists also refer to as the vertebral column, is the body's main means of support. The superior end of the spinal column supports the skull, while the bottom links up with the pelvis (the hips). For the most part it's flexible, allowing a person to bend over, for example, but it's also quite strong.

The spinal column is made up of thirty-three separate bones called vertebrae. Anatomists like to divide these bones into five distinct spinal groups: the cervical spine, the thoracic spine, the lumbar spine, the sacral spine, and the coccyx. The cervical spine is what most people know as the neck. It consists of the first seven vertebrae, which, for identification purposes, are often numbered C1 through C7. C1 is at the very superior end of the spinal column and supports the skull.

Directly below the cervical spine is the thoracic spine. The thoracic spine is essentially the upper back and includes twelve thoracic vertebrae, numbered T1 through T12. The thoracic region coincides with the ribs. Below the thoracic spine are the five vertebrae of the lumbar spine (L1 through L5), or lower back. The muscles near the lumbar spine are often injured by people who lift heavy objects. In adult humans, the spinal cord's inferior end, called the conus medullaris, is between L1 and L2. Next comes the sacral spine, which consists of five vertebrae (S1 through S5) fused together to form one platelike bone known as the sacrum. The sacrum can be felt as the rigid bone on the back of your pelvis.

The last three to five vertebrae (the number varies from person to person) of the spinal column are also fused together into one curvy bone. This bone is called the coccyx, or tailbone. If you're reclined on a sofa as you read this, you're probably resting on your coccyx.

Each vertebra is separated from those above and below it by fluid-filled cushions of sturdy elastic cartilage called intervertebral discs. The discs serve as built-in shock absorbers for the spine. Their elasticity also permits the

Thirty-three vertebrae give the spinal column its strength and flexibility.

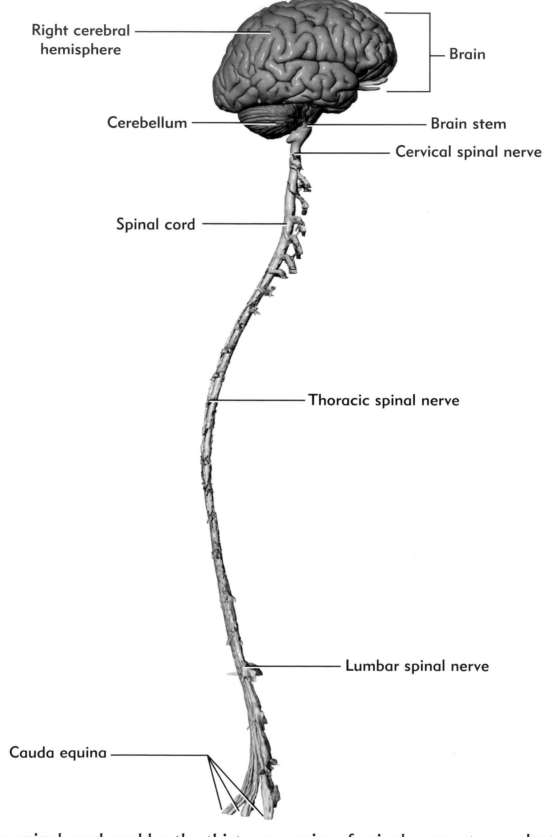

Right cerebral hemisphere

Brain

Cerebellum

Brain stem

Cervical spinal nerve

Spinal cord

Thoracic spinal nerve

Lumbar spinal nerve

Cauda equina

The spinal cord enables the thirty-one pairs of spinal nerves to conduct information from the body to the brain, and vice versa.

spine to move. Without them, our backs would be stiff and unmovable, like a metal pole. Spinal disc injuries from heavy lifting or over-twisting of the back are very common. But it's better to slip a disc than it is to harm what's hidden inside it.

The Spinal Cord

The average length of the spinal cord in an adult man is forty-five centimeters. In adult women it tends to be a little bit shorter—about forty-two centimeters. It's anywhere from six to twelve millimeters wide, depending on where you measure it, but in general, the farther down the spinal column it goes, the narrower it gets.

The spinal cord serves as the central pipeline for thirty-one different pairs of spinal nerves (eight cervical, twelve thoracic, five lumbar, five sacral, and one coccygeal). The spinal nerves act like conductors for information traveling to and from the spinal cord to the rest of the body. The anatomy is extremely complex. Protruding from the spinal cord are spinal roots. The spinal roots attach to spinal nerves. The spinal nerves then split into ventral and dorsal (front and back) rami. Finally, the rami, which contain threadlike nervous fibers, branch out to the rest of the body. To simplify, imagine the spinal nerves as two rows of thirty-one trees planted along a strip of ground. The strip of ground is the spinal cord, the tree trunks are the spinal nerves, and the tree branches are the rami. The rami branches reach far and wide to every corner of the human body, including the legs, arms, hands, and feet.

With the exception of the very first spinal nerve, C-1, spinal nerves exit the spinal column between vertebrae. For example, spinal nerve C-2 exits the spinal cord between vertebrae C1 and C2, and spinal nerve C-8 exits between vertebrae C7 and T1. C-1, the oddball, exits between the C1 vertebra, which is also known as the atlas (the word

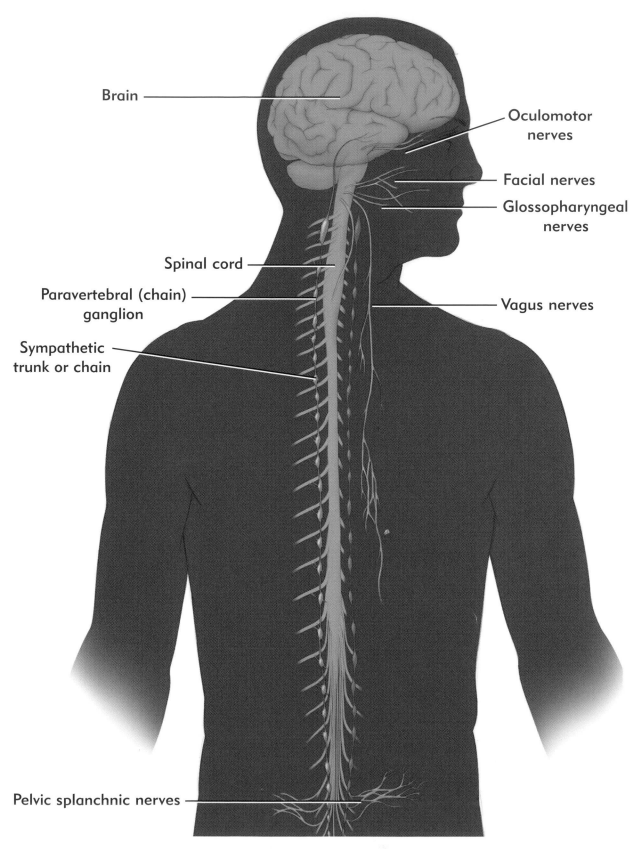

Brain

Oculomotor nerves

Facial nerves

Glossopharyngeal nerves

Spinal cord

Paravertebral (chain) ganglion

Vagus nerves

Sympathetic trunk or chain

Pelvic splanchnic nerves

The brain, spinal cord, nerves, and receptors are part of the nervous system, which enables the body to control its actions.

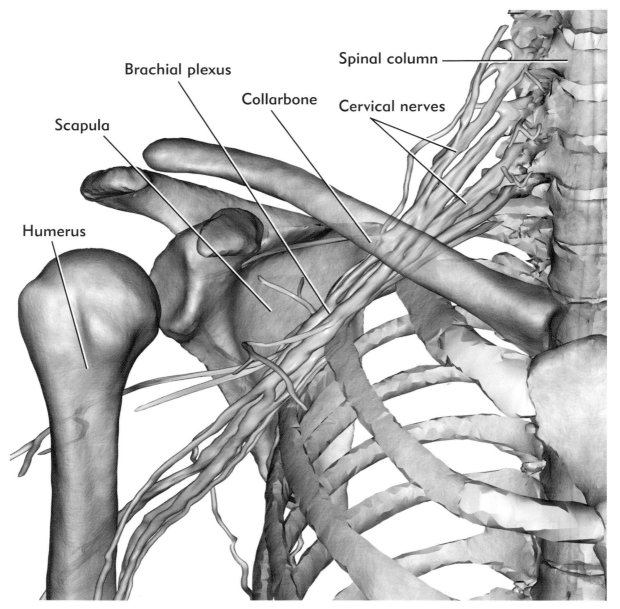

Scapula

Humerus

Brachial plexus

Collarbone

Spinal column

Cervical nerves

A bundle of cervical nerves branches out from the spinal column near the shoulder.

"atlas" comes from the hero of Greek mythology who held the world on his shoulders), and the occipital bone of the skull, which rests on top of the atlas. The thoracic, lumbar, and sacral nerves of the spinal cord exit the spinal column below the vertebrae of the same number. So spinal nerve L-1, for example, exits between the L1 and L2 vertebrae. And spinal nerve S-1 exits between the S1 and S2 vertebrae.

The spinal cord is much shorter than the spinal column, so spinal nerves near the inferior end of the cord, especially the lumbar and sacral nerves, must travel down the column for some distance before they can exit between vertebrae. Picture spinal nerve S-2, for instance. It enters the spinal column at about the same level as the L1 vertebrae but exits between the S2 and S3 vertebrae. So it has to travel down the column just to get out. As a result, there is a tail-like collection of nerves near the inferior end of the spinal column that anatomists call the cauda equina, which is Latin for "horse's tail."

Protection of the Spinal Cord

Like the brain, the spinal cord is protected by three layers of meninges—the dura mater, the arachnoid, and the pia mater—and circulating cerebrospinal fluid. The meninges travel most of the length of the spinal column, continuing far past the inferior end of the spinal cord in the lumbar area to form a baglike meningeal sac in the sacral area. Doctors often "tap" this sac to collect and test samples of the cerebrospinal fluid inside it for certain diseases.

Another major guard against spinal cord injury is, not surprisingly, the vertebrae of the spinal column. Vertebrae come in all different sizes, but their basic structure is the same. The main part of the bone is called the vertebral body. It makes the spinal column strong. Attached to the vertebral body is the vertebral arch, which surrounds and protects the spinal cord like a personal bodyguard. Protruding from the vertebral arch are various finlike processes. The processes do things like attach to back muscles, restrict potentially dangerous movements, and prevent vertebral discs from slipping.

3
THOUGHT AND EMOTION

While scientists certainly know a lot about the brain and the spinal cord and the functions of each, the role they play in our experience of emotions—feelings of love, happiness, anger, fear, sadness, and excitement—can get a little confusing. In fact, until recently, many researchers considered emotions to be so different from person to person that they thought scientific studies of the subject would be useless and inaccurate. How could you ever claim love, for instance, was an identical experience from one person to the next? As a result, relatively little serious research was ever conducted.

Today, however, attitudes about emotions have changed. High-tech brain-scanning tools are now being used to figure out exactly what parts of the brain play the biggest role in the emotional realm. By studying the unique pathways that different emotions follow through the brain, scientists have discovered that no one part of the brain is entirely responsible for how we experience those emotions. Emotions are processed by almost every area of the brain, they say. Our bodies respond to life's emotional experiences in many different ways, both physically and mentally, and our personal responses to those experiences are a result of everything coming together in the brain.

Interestingly, using these scanning techniques, scientists now know why emotions can affect a person's ability to think. When we

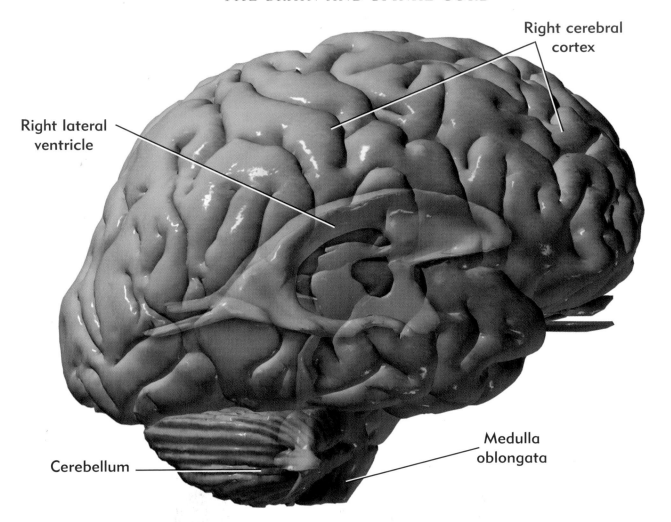

Right cerebral cortex

Right lateral ventricle

Cerebellum

Medulla oblongata

This lateral (side) view of the brain shows the ventricle and the medulla oblongata. The ventricles filter and create cerebrospinal fluid.

experience extreme emotions, like an intense feeling of love for some-one close to us, the flurry of neural activity that results affects the brain like a severe internal electrical storm. The interference prevents the brain from interpreting new information—from thinking.

The Limbic System

While many areas of the brain play a role in our emotions, the limbic system is definitely the most important. In fact, the limbic system is so important in producing emotions that it's often referred to as the "emotional brain."

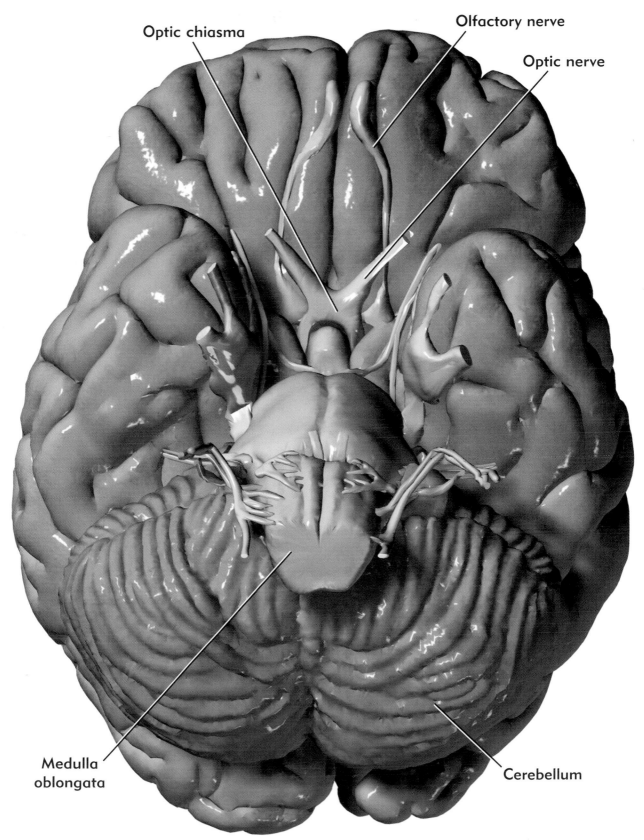

Optic chiasma

Olfactory nerve

Optic nerve

Medulla
oblongata

Cerebellum

This ventral (bottom) view of the brain reveals the cerebellum and the
cranial nerves.

Human emotions can result from a specific thought or from a message delivered to the brain from sensory organs (triggered by something you see, smell, taste, touch, or hear). Both situations create nerve impulses that travel to the limbic system. There, depending on what the message or thought is, the impulses kick different parts of the limbic system into gear. The system, in turn, produces emotions. Good or bad, it all depends on the information the limbic system receives.

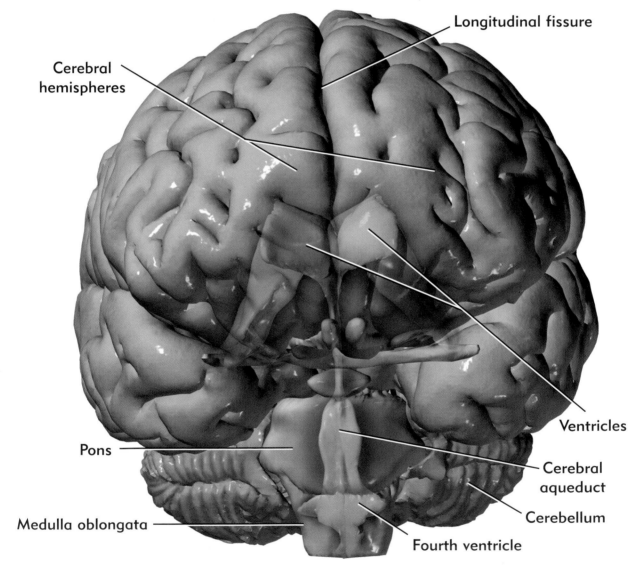

The cerebellum helps to control the body's balance and to coordinate the contractions of the muscles for smooth movements.

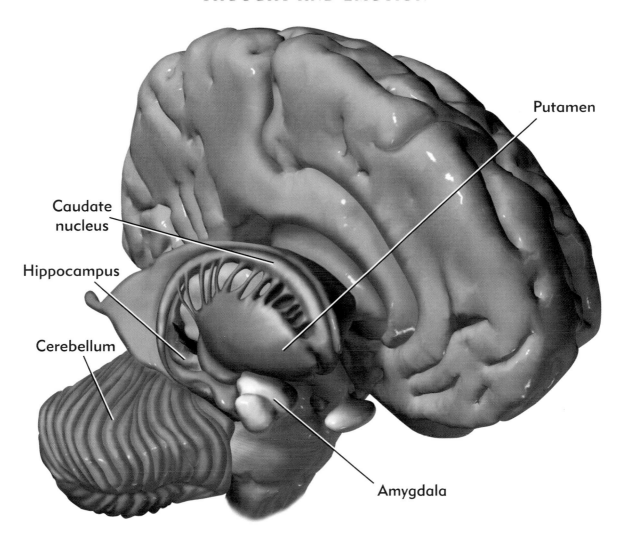

Putamen

Caudate
nucleus

Hippocampus

Cerebellum

Amygdala

With the right hemisphere of the cerebral cortex removed, the parts of the limbic system can be seen clearly. The limbic system adds emotions to our thoughts.

The limbic system is made up of two main parts: the cortical region and the subcortical region. Within the cortical region is the hippocampus. One of the things the hippocampus influences is the release of a hormone from the body's adrenal gland that affects moods and behaviors. For example, in times of stress—like when you're worried about a tough test that is coming up—this natural substance, known as corticosteroid hormone, enters your bloodstream.

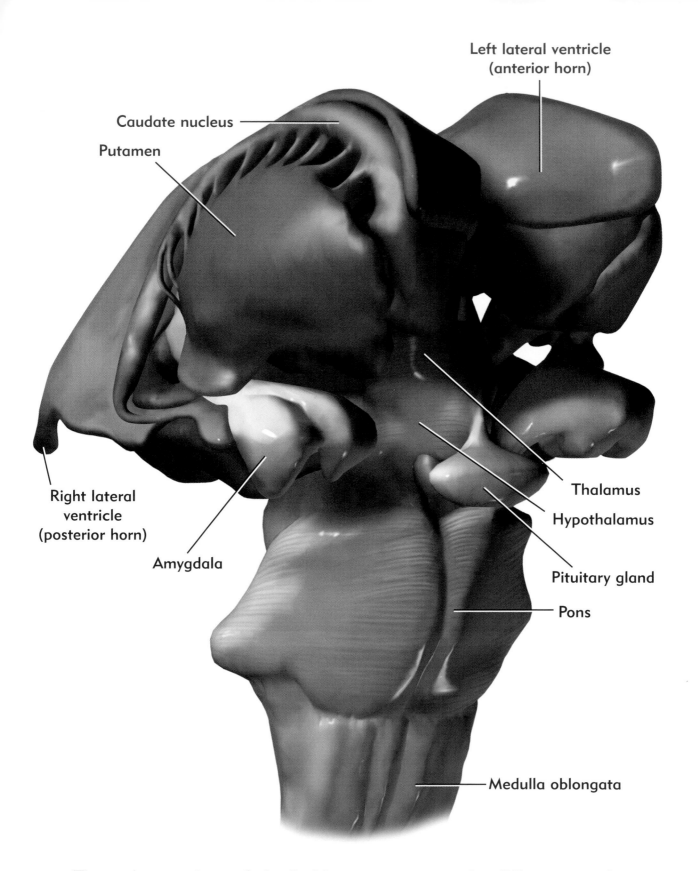

Left lateral ventricle
(anterior horn)

Caudate nucleus

Putamen

Right lateral
ventricle
(posterior horn)

Amygdala

Thalamus

Hypothalamus

Pituitary gland

Pons

Medulla oblongata

The various regions of the limbic system govern the different emotions we experience, such as fear, pleasure, and anger.

In the subcortical region, three parts in particular play major roles in emotions. One part is the septum, also known as the brain's pleasure center. This is where the brain recognizes certain sensations as pleasurable.

The subcortical region's amygdala, on the other hand, regulates emotions like fear, arousal, and anger. The amygdala is located in the temporal lobe of the brain. One of the main jobs of the amygdala is to create connections between stimuli and their emotional value (whether a particular stimulus is good or bad). This occurs through memories, which almost always include an emotional aspect. If deep in your mind you remember that a certain incident made you sad, for instance, the next time a similar incident occurs your brain will tell you to be sad again. In scientific experiments, wild animals with damaged amygdalas lose their fear of potentially dangerous predators and humans.

The last main part of the subcortical region of the limbic system is called the hypothalamus. "Hypothalamus" means "under the thalamus," and that's exactly where it's located—at the base of the diencephalon, inferior to the thalamus. The hypothalamus does a lot of things, but its primary function is to regulate emotions such as anger, pain, pleasure, sexual feelings, and survival instincts, such as the desire for food and water. An animal with a damaged hypothalamus might even forget to eat and starve to death. The hypothalamus also regulates the pituitary gland, which hangs from the hypothalamus and secretes several hormones that control important bodily functions.

Thought and Memory

Much like the anatomy of emotions, thinking and memory involve extremely complex brain activities. Scientists are still deciphering how thoughts work, and they're learning new things every day.

Interpreting Emotions

Thanks to neuroscientists at the University of Iowa, we now know that the right prefrontal cortex, a region at the front of the brain's right hemisphere, is the part of the brain that allows us to recognize and interpret the facial expressions of other people. During a rare surgical operation in which the scientists inserted special depth electrodes into their patient's brain while he was awake, they were able to see that neurons in the right prefrontal cortex were activated as he was shown photographs of strangers with unique facial expressions and interpreted those emotions. So, next time you see someone frown and you know that they're sad, or watch a person smile and are sure that they're happy, thank your brain—the right prefrontal cortex of your brain, that is.

When we think, we form, create, or process something in our mind. We ponder the solution to a problem, we imagine ourselves in a different place, or we remember something from long ago. One part of the brain known to play a role in thought is the association cortex of the cerebrum, in the frontal lobes. The brain's association areas give us our intellectual abilities, our ability to reason and to make plans, and our language and communication skills. They also influence how smart we are, what kind of personality we have, and our decision-making abilities. They allow us to imagine what might happen should we do something before we actually do it. They permit us to understand why someone might feel a particular way and what their reasons are for doing certain things. Scientists have found that people with

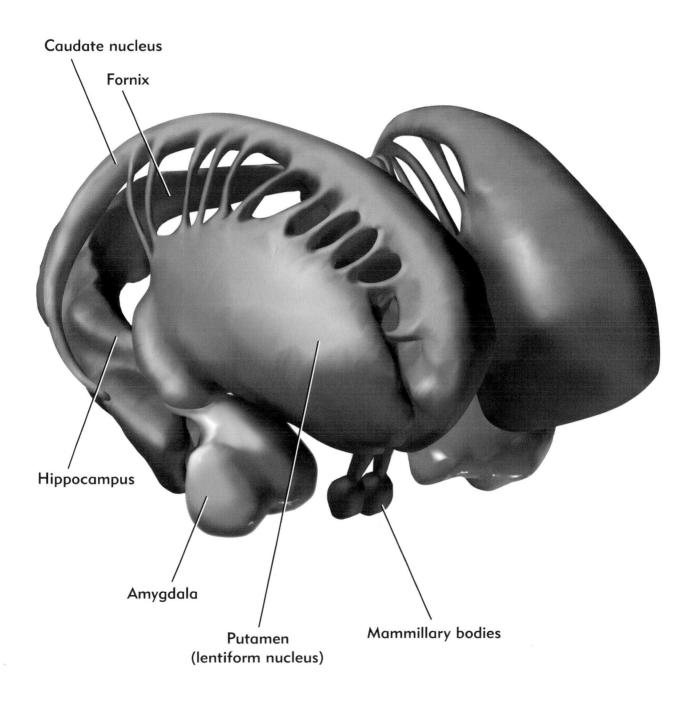

Caudate nucleus

Fornix

Hippocampus

Amygdala

Putamen
(lentiform nucleus)

Mammillary bodies

These are parts of the limbic system. Because of the limbic system, our thoughts are often associated with strong feelings.

damaged frontal lobes lose the ability to think and reason in these ways. They often act in strange, socially unacceptable ways and their emotional reactions to certain situations become very unpredictable.

The way thought works is complex. Information gathered from the senses enters the association cortex, is interpreted and processed, and is combined—or associated—with information that is already stored in memory. The more abstract and difficult the ideas or subjects the brain tries to process, the more complex that processing becomes. Learning and memory take place primarily in the hippocampus, which, as mentioned earlier, is a part of the limbic system. Scientists believe the hippocampus acts like a storage center for memories and helps people to form new memories.

Another region of the brain involved in memory are the mammillary bodies of the hypothalamus. The mammillary bodies, which are reflex centers important for the sense of smell, sprout like miniature antennae from the floor of the hypothalamus. Damage to the mammillary bodies can result in severe memory loss—a condition called Korsakov's syndrome.

4
THE NERVOUS SYSTEM

The human nervous system—which includes the brain, the spinal cord, and countless nerves and receptors for every limb, organ, and muscle—is the body's way of talking to itself and controlling its actions. It allows the body to respond to stimuli from the outside world like light, sound, and heat. It also permits the body to react to internal changes, such as decreasing oxygen levels, for example.

The nervous system communicates with the rest of the body by sending rapid electrical impulses to specific body parts. In order to know what signals to send, the nervous system does three things. First, it relies on millions of tiny sensory receptors to sense changes occurring both inside and outside of the body. Second, it takes the information gathered by the receptors, called sensory input, figures out what that information means, and decides what to do about it. Finally, with a decision in hand, the nervous system responds to the sensory input with motor output—a reaction. Two examples of motor output are the movement of a muscle and the secretion of sweat or saliva from glands.

The CNS and the PNS

There are two major parts to the human nervous system: the central nervous system and the peripheral nervous system. The central nervous system, or CNS, consists of the brain and spinal cord. Together, the

Optic chiasma

Optic
nerves

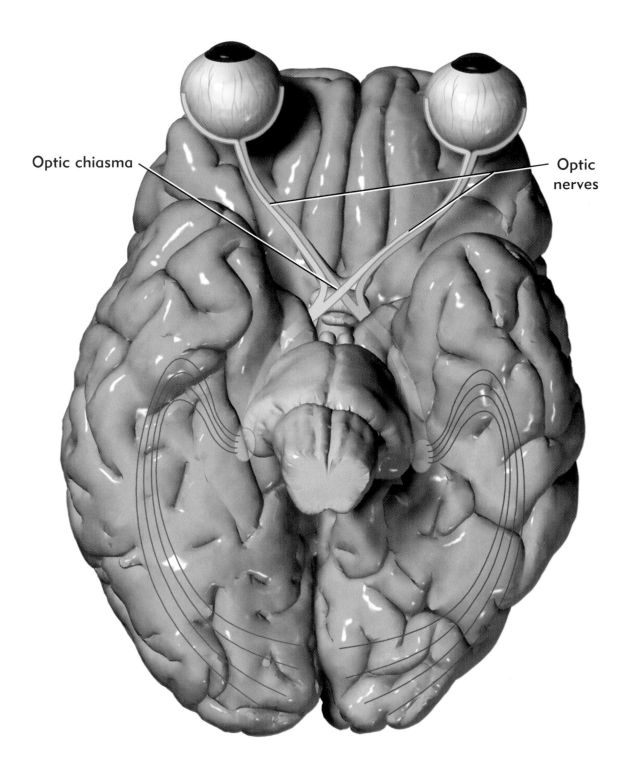

The two optic nerves cross over at the optic chiasma, so the right side of
the brain interprets images from the left eye, and vice versa.

brain and spinal cord serve as the nervous system's command station. When sensory input arrives at the CNS, the brain and spinal cord figure out exactly what it means. Then, almost instantaneously, they fire orders out to the body parts that need to be mobilized.

Everything outside of the central nervous system is known as the peripheral nervous system, or PNS. The PNS includes all the nerves that leave the brain and spinal cord and travel to various parts of the body. The nerves carrying information in the form of nerve impulses to and from the brain are called cranial nerves. Those that carry nerve impulses to and from the spine are called spinal nerves. The peripheral nervous system's main job is to send information gathered from the body's sensory receptors as quickly as possible to the central nervous system. Then, once the CNS has interpreted that information, the PNS instantly relays specific orders back out to the body.

There are two main parts to the peripheral nervous system. The first part is the sensory division. The sensory division is like the body's incoming post office. It collects impulses from sensory receptors in places like the skin, muscles, and organs, and carries those impulses through nerves to the central nervous system. The second main part of the peripheral nervous system is the motor division. The motor division has the opposite job of the sensory division. It collects the outgoing messages from the central nervous system and delivers them to the appropriate body organs, effectively telling them exactly what to do.

The motor division itself can be divided into two parts: the autonomic nervous system and the somatic nervous system. The autonomic nervous system is responsible for controlling automatic body functions—those activities of the body we have no conscious control over, like the everyday beating of the heart. Our autonomic nervous system often kicks in when we experience stressful things like severe

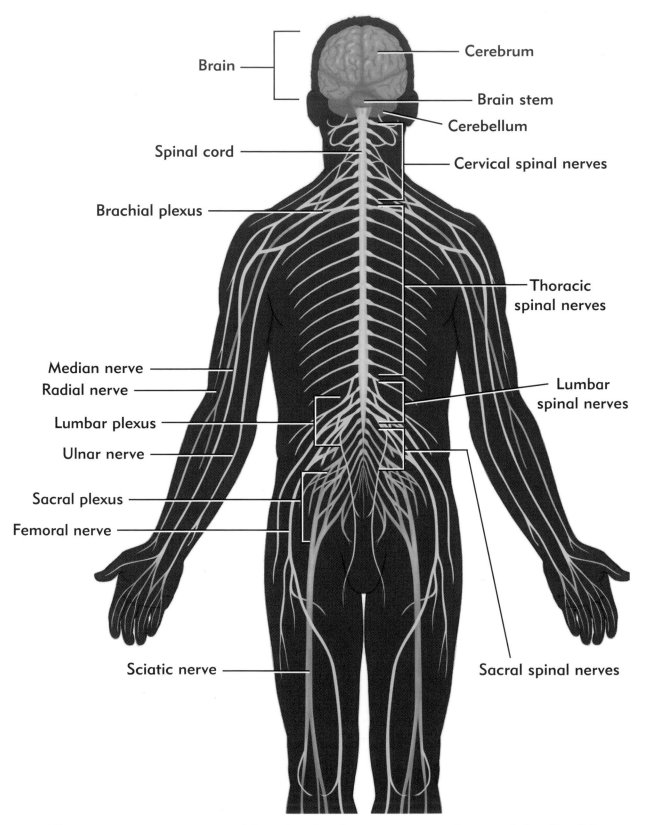

Brain

Cerebrum

Brain stem

Cerebellum

Spinal cord

Cervical spinal nerves

Brachial plexus

Thoracic spinal nerves

Median nerve

Radial nerve

Lumbar spinal nerves

Lumbar plexus

Ulnar nerve

Sacral plexus

Femoral nerve

Sciatic nerve

Sacral spinal nerves

The nervous system enables the body to communicate with all of its parts and to respond to sensory experiences from the outside world, such as light, sound, and heat.

injury, blood loss, or fright. Not surprisingly, the autonomic nervous system is also known as the involuntary nervous system. The somatic nervous system, on the other hand, is responsible for our voluntary movements—those muscle movements we consciously decide we would like to make. Another name for the somatic nervous system is the voluntary nervous system.

Neurons, Axons, and Synapses

The nervous system is made of two types of cells. Nerve cells, known as neurons, are cells of the nervous system that transmit messages throughout the body. Neurons consist of nerve bodies, which receive stimuli, and threadlike nerve processes—or axons—which carry the stimuli to other neurons and to organs. Neurons respond to stimuli with an electrical discharge called a nerve impulse from a receptor, and then conduct that nerve impulse along a chain of neurons all the way to the brain.

Neurons are very close to one another, but they do not touch. Instead, there's a space between each one called a synapse through which information is transmitted by means of chemicals known as neurotransmitters. Information is passed through one neuron, transmitted through a synaptic cleft, and then picked up by the next neuron, and then the process is repeated.

The second type of cells, glial cells, are so-called supporting cells. They help the neurons do their job. For instance, some glial cells lay down a substance called myelin (a fat layer) that allows the electrical impulse to travel faster. Other glial cells defend neurons by attacking bacteria and dangerous foreign substances. There are far more glial cells in the nervous system than there are neurons, but that should be expected. One can never have too many helpers, after all.

White Matter and Gray Matter

If you were to take a knife and carve a slice out of the brain, the inside surface of the resulting sliver of nervous tissue would be colored both white and gray. The white, centrally located areas are known as white matter. The gray areas near the outside, in the cortex, are called gray matter and consist of neuronal cell bodies. White matter is made of

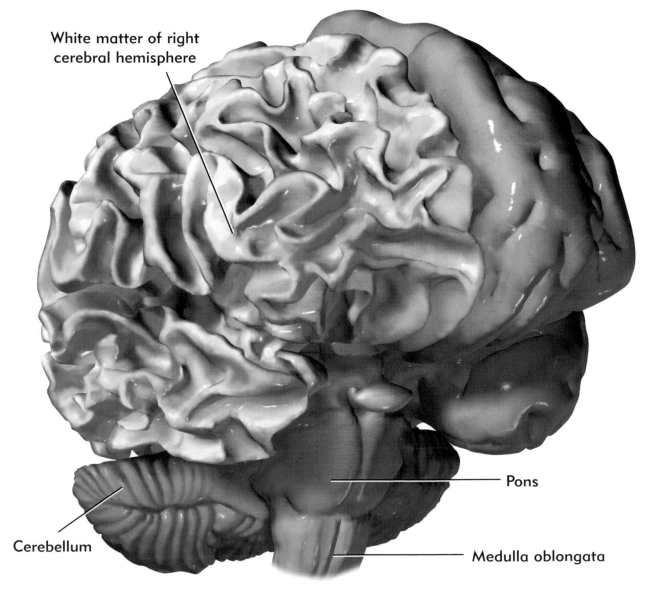

White matter of right cerebral hemisphere

Pons

Cerebellum

Medulla oblongata

The brain's white matter, underlying the gray matter of the cerebral cortex, is composed of axons, which are threadlike fibers that conduct nerve impulses.

axons, the threadlike fibers that branch away from the neuronal cell bodies and conduct nerve impulses. The axons get their white color from myelin, a fatty material that forms a protective and insulating sheath around them.

Like the brain, the spinal cord is also composed of gray matter and white matter. Snip it in two and the gray and white sections can be seen by the naked eye. The outer part of the cord is made of white matter, while the central part—shaped like an H—is made of gray matter. Again, spinal cord white matter consists of axons that carry signals to and from the brain, and spinal cord gray matter consists of neuronal cell bodies.

Reflexes

A reflex is an automatic nervous system response to a stimulus. Reflexes occur whether we want them to or not. We are born with them; our bodies are ready to use them from the very second we come into the world. Most reflexes are very important for everyday functioning. We use them all the time. For example, we have reflexes for swallowing and blinking. Some reflexes can be controlled. For instance, we have reflexes that make us want to urinate, but we can usually prevent ourselves from urinating until we find a bathroom.

There are two types of reflexes: autonomic reflexes and somatic reflexes. Autonomic reflexes control things like digestion, urination, sweating, and blood pressure. Somatic reflexes are reflexes that control skeletal muscles. For example, when you touch your tongue to a cup of scorching hot water, a somatic reflex makes you quickly pull away—hopefully before you burn yourself. The path a reflex follows through the nervous system is called a reflex arc.

GLOSSARY

autonomic nervous system   The body system responsible for controlling automatic body functions, like breathing and swallowing.

axons   Strands of nerve tissue that carry information to neurons and organs.

central nervous system   The part of the nervous system that includes the brain and the spinal cord.

cerebrospinal fluid   A clear, waterlike substance that circulates within the subarachnoid space of the brain and spinal cord.

emotions   Feelings such as happiness, sadness, anger, and fear.

gray matter   Gray regions of the brain and spinal cord consisting of neuronal cell bodies.

limbic system   Brain-based system that scientists believe is important for processing emotions.

membrane   Thin layer of body tissue.

meninges   Layers of tissue that protect the brain and the spinal cord.

motor output   Body's reaction to stimuli.

nerve fibers   Threadlike strands of nerves that transmit information.

nerve impulse   Electrical discharge from a neuron that is conducted to the brain.

nervous system   Body system that includes the brain, spinal cord, nerves, and receptors, and that controls both voluntary and involuntary actions.

peripheral nervous system   Part of the nervous system outside of the brain and spinal cord.

receptor   Cell or group of cells that senses stimuli from inside or outside of the body.

reflex   Automatic nervous system response to a stimulus.

sensory input   Information gathered by body receptors and transmitted to the central nervous system.

somatic nervous system   Body system responsible for voluntary movements.

synapse   Space between two neurons through which information is transmitted.

tissue   Collection of cells that forms a structural material of the body.

vascular system   Body system consisting of various channels that circulate blood.

ventricles   Chambers inside the brain that produce and circulate cerebrospinal fluid.

vertebral column   Spinal column, consisting of thirty-three vertebrae and intervertebral discs.

white matter   White regions of the brain and spinal cord consisting of axons.

FOR MORE INFORMATION

American Academy of Neurology
1080 Montreal Avenue
St. Paul, MN 55116
(651) 695-1940
Web site: http://www.aan.com

American Medical Association
515 North State Street
Chicago, IL 60610
(312) 464-5000
Web site: http://www.ama-assn.org

Society for Neuroscience
11 Dupont Circle NW, Suite 500
Washington, DC 20036
(202) 462-6688
Web site: http://www.sfn.org

Web Sites

American Association of Anatomists
http://www.anatomy.org/anatomy/nresource.htm
A very long list of anatomy resources available on the Internet.

Anatomy-Resources.com

http://www.anatomy-resources.com

A great place to find cool anatomy books and models of body parts, skeletons, and organs.

BodyQuest

http://Library.thinkquest.org/10348/home.html

Tour the virtual human body and learn all about its different systems.

HealthWeb

http://www.healthweb.org

Links to the best health information available on the Internet.

Neuroanatomy and Neuropathology on the Internet

http://www.neuropat.dote.hu

A searchable and browseable directory. It's intended for medical students and medical professionals, but it has lots of links.

Neuroscience for Kids

http://faculty.washington.edu/chudler/neurok.html

Easy-to-understand information on the brain and spinal cord.

Neurosciences on the Internet

http://www.neuroguide.com

An extensive collection of neuroscience resources available on the Internet.

FOR FURTHER READING

Alcamo, Edward. *Anatomy and Physiology the Easy Way*. Hauppauge, NY: Barrons Educational Series, 1996.

Barmeier, Jim. *The Brain*. San Diego, CA: Lucent Books, 1996.

Barrett, Susan. *It's All in Your Head: A Guide to Understanding Your Brain and Boosting Your Brain Power*. Minneapolis, MN: Free Spirit Publishing, 1992.

Clayman, Charles. *Illustrated Guide to the Human Body*. New York: DK Publishing, 1995.

Kapit, Wynn. *The Anatomy Coloring Book*. Reading, MA: Addison-Wesley Publishing Company, 1993.

Pinel, John. *A Colorful Introduction to the Anatomy of the Human Brain: A Brain and Psychology Coloring Book*. Needham Heights, MA: Allyn & Bacon, 1997.

Simon, Seymour. *The Brain: Our Nervous System*. New York: William Morrow & Company, 1997.

Treays, Rebecca. *Understanding Your Brain*. Tulsa, OK: EDC Publications, 1996.

INDEX

About the Author

Chris Hayhurst is an emergency medical technician, professional author, and journalist with more than a dozen books and hundreds of articles in print. He lives and works in Fort Collins, Colorado.

Photo Credits

All digital images courtesy of Visible Productions, by arrangement with Anatographica, LLC.

Series Design

Claudia Carlson

Layout

Tahara Hasan